BOLD KIDS

Puerto Rico

CHILDREN'S BOOK FILLED WITH FACTS

No part of this book may be reproduced or used in any way or form or by any means whether electronic or mechanical, this means that you cannot record or photocopy any material ideas or tips that are provided in this book.
Copyright 2022

All images in this book have been reproduced with the knowledge and prior consent of the artists concerned, and no responsibility is accepted by producer, publisher, or printer for any infringement of copyright or otherwise, arising from the contents of this publication.

Children who are studying the history of Puerto Rico will be thrilled to discover the fascinating places and interesting facts of this island country. The Caribbean archipelago country is home to many beautiful islands and a rich culture.

Its geography makes it an important place for kids to study. Here are some fun facts about Puerto Rico for kids. You'll learn the island's history, geography, animals, and climate. These are all interesting facts to share with your child.

The first Spanish settlers in the Americas arrived in the early 1500s, bringing with them the language and culture of the island. They settled in the city of San Juan, which is known for its casinos, beach bars, and casino.

The people of the island are friendly, open, and passionate. They also express their feelings with great intensity. In addition to a rich history, Puerto Rico is home to the world's largest radio telescope.

The island has a robust road network, covering more than 16,000 miles (22,400 kilometers). The road network is best developed in the area around San Juan. The island also has a rapid transit system, called Tren Urbano, which serves the city of San Juan as well as parts of the surrounding suburbs.

Aside from roads, Puerto Rico also has a thriving transportation system, which includes ferries and buses.

Puerto Rico is the largest unincorporated territory in the US and is located in the northeast Caribbean Sea. It is home to a variety of colorful, natural, and historical sites. The islands are mostly land-based, though it has a rich wildlife ecosystem.

Some of the most famous species include the African tulip tree and royal poinciana. There are a variety of birds and mammals, including the coqui, a tiny frog that sings a high-pitched song at night.

There are many places to visit in Puerto Rico, including the capital city of San Juan. There are a number of places to visit in San Juan, and there are numerous museums and galleries. It's also worth mentioning that the island has a dual language system.

Distances, speed, and the measure of food are all measured in miles per hour. The official language is Spanish, but English was introduced during the Spanish-American War, and is used primarily in the interior.

The island is home to more than 200 species of birds, including the endangered green Puerto Rican parrot. It also has a number of land animals, including nonpoisonous snakes and lizards. The island's native frog, the coqui, is also a national mascot.

Fish and shellfish are abundant in Puerto Rico, although mixed species limits commercial fishing. The islands' natural resources are diverse and are a great place to raise children.

Aside from the stunning beaches, Puerto Rico also has some of the most amazing natural wonders in the Caribbean. It is the only island in the United States to have two oceans, so if your child wants to learn about this amazing place, he or she will enjoy learning facts about it.

This is a great way to introduce kids to the wonders of the country. If you're planning a trip to the island, don't miss out on the unique beauty of the area.

There are more than 200 species of birds in Puerto Rico. One of the most fascinating of these is the small green Puerto Rican parrot, which is considered a national symbol. Other animals in the island include nonpoisonous snakes, lizards, and monkeys.

Aside from these, the native frog, the coqui, is also a national mascot. While fish are plentiful in the waters of the island, commercial fishing is restricted due to its mixed species.

While there are many interesting places to see in Puerto Rico, it is a great place for families to spend a family vacation. The beautiful beaches of the island are sure to delight your family. However, the rusted military tanks on Culebra Island are a fun way to show your kids the historical significance of the area.

There are also several WWII-era forts on the island. As you can see, Puerto Rico is a popular vacation spot for families and tourists alike.

Ingram Content Group UK Ltd.
Milton Keynes UK
UKHW050241260723
425736UK00009B/27